# THE SLOW-RIPENING FRUITS OF *Mothering*

# THE SLOW-RIPENING FRUITS OF *Mothering*

**EMILY WATTS**

DESERET BOOK

Salt Lake City, Utah

© 2013 Emily Watts

All rights reserved. No part of this book may be reproduced in any form or by any means without permission in writing from the publisher, Deseret Book Company, at permissions@deseretbook.com or P. O. Box 30178, Salt Lake City, Utah 84130. This work is not an official publication of The Church of Jesus Christ of Latter-day Saints. The views expressed herein are the responsibility of the author and do not necessarily represent the position of the Church or of Deseret Book Company.

DESERET BOOK is a registered trademark of Deseret Book Company.

Visit us at DeseretBook.com

**Library of Congress Cataloging-in-Publication Data**
Watts, Emily, author.
 The slow-ripening fruits of mothering / Emily Watts.
    pages cm
 Includes bibliographical references.
 ISBN 978-1-60907-712-9 (hardbound : alk. paper)  1. Motherhood—Religious aspects—The Church of Jesus Christ of Latter-day Saints. I. Title.
 BX8643.W66W38 2013
 248.8'431—dc23                                                      2013019709

Printed in the United States of America
R. R. Donnelley, Crawfordsville, IN

10  9  8  7  6  5  4  3  2  1

*For Larry*
*Fellow gardener in the family orchard*

*I* am not fond of flying. Time Out for Women takes us as speakers all over the country, and sometimes we end up on really small planes. As I am not a really small woman, some of these planes get pretty claustrophobic. I've been on planes I could not even stand upright in. Getting to my seat on such a plane is like crawling into a cave to begin with, and then when I finally settle in, I'm squinched with my knees up against the pocket of the seat in front of me the whole time. At least I understand why they can't provide more legroom on those tiny planes. What I don't understand is why the seat belts also seem proportionately smaller. On a regular-sized plane, I can fasten a (fully extended) seat belt with no problem, but on a "puddle-jumper" I feel like I'm being cut in half. And I'll be hanged if I'll ask for a seat-belt extender! I have *some* pride.

Anyway, flying is not my favorite thing, but there is one thing I like about it, and that is the chance to peruse the *SkyMall* magazine. Shopping in the air is such a fun concept to begin with—and the *SkyMall* magazine is a catalog unlike any other catalog I know. It is filled with things I've never seen in a store, little luxuries that will always exceed my budget and rarely speak to my actual needs, but that I love looking at just to see what those inventive people have come up with.

One of the things I most enjoy is reading the headlines, because I know the headline is always carefully crafted to try to draw you in and capture your interest in the product. So I usually leaf through and peruse the headlines, just seeing what catches my eye. A particular favorite of mine said,

## THE SLOW-RIPENING FRUITS OF MOTHERING

"Now Unsightly Sock Lines Can Be a Thing of the Past!" I was intrigued and even a little excited over the existence of such a product despite the fact that I am not quite sure what an unsightly sock line *is*. In my world, the unsightly sock line is where the hem of your dress fails to come down far enough to meet the top of your knee-high nylons. That is unsightly, I grant you.

But no: apparently, an unsightly sock line is what happens when you are careless enough to go out in the sun for an extended period with ankle socks on. When you come inside to discover that your legs are all tan and your feet are still white, that's an unsightly sock line. I'm sure that's genuinely a problem for some people, although not for one such as I, whose legs have not seen direct sunlight for probably ten or fifteen years (and you don't want them to at this point).

The remedy, in case you wonder, for the unsightly sock line is a device called the Tootsie Tanner. I did not make this up. The Tootsie Tanner is a little mini-sunlamp that you can put your feet under to toast away those sock lines. To me this seems fraught with peril because what if you get it wrong? What if you get your foot under a little bit too far and you have a band where the tans overlap? *That's* unsightly. Or if you get your feet too tan, do you put your socks back on and go out in the sun to even things back out? I just could not see how that process would work, so I did not purchase the Tootsie Tanner, in spite of the intriguing headline.

Here is another great headline I saw in the *SkyMall* magazine: "Dine with Children Worry-Free." Immediately upon seeing that, I thought, *I must have this product*. What could it be? What could they be offering that would allow one to "Dine with children worry-free"? Was it some kind of soundproof cubicle so that you didn't have to listen to the kids complaining about the food?

Child: "I don't like this."

Mom: "You've never even tasted it."

## THE SLOW-RIPENING FRUITS OF MOTHERING

Child: "That's why I don't like it. I only like things I've tasted."

Mom: "Fine. I'll nurse you for the rest of your life." (For the record, Mom probably doesn't say this last line out loud.)

Or if the solution were not a soundproof cubicle, perhaps it would be blinders, so that child A can't see that child B got an extra dinosaur chicken nugget on his plate. No, no, no. You can't rely on an outside vendor for that. You have to be more careful about counting. When I became a mother, I became an obsessive counter. When I filled plastic Easter eggs, not only did I count Skittles, I counted to be sure each child had the same number of red Skittles, the same number of green Skittles, the same number of yellow Skittles, and so on, because they taste different, and we have to be *fair*. Now, of course, I realize how futile and stupid that was because I have one relatively OCD child who would line up all her Skittles according to color while her brother next to her would be upending the egg right into his mouth and dumping them all in at once. He didn't know if she had more; he was just trying to control that rainbow drool. But for years I counted Skittles.

Anyway, just so you know, to dine with children worry-free, what *SkyMall* magazine says you need is plastic seat covers for your upholstered dining-room chairs. To which I say, "Have these people ever *been* in a home with children?" Who thinks it's a good idea to have upholstered dining room chairs in a house where children dump whole eggsful of Skittles into their mouths at one time? But we must preserve appearances, and that is what most of the products in the *SkyMall* magazine are for. Indeed, a good percentage of the products that we purchase in today's world are designed to help us keep up appearances.

I don't want you to believe that I don't think appearance is important. Appearance can provide vital clues for our interactions with one another. For example, if we see two clean-cut young men walking down the street in dark suits and white shirts and black name tags, we automatically draw some

## THE SLOW-RIPENING FRUITS OF MOTHERING

assumptions about them. Even people who are not acquainted with our missionary program would be more likely to open a door to young men looking like that than they would to a couple of young men looking like most college students do these days.

*A good percentage of the products that we purchase in today's world are designed to help us keep up appearances.*

In general conference, if one of the Brethren were to stand up to speak to us in a polo shirt, would we not be alarmed? I don't care if he's the newest General Authority on the block—nobody had to call him and say, "Be sure to wear a white shirt." Because of the solemnity of that occasion, it's pretty clear what kind of attire is appropriate for it. Appearance can be an outward manifestation of an inward

*Sometimes we get so busy working out the appearance part of our lives that we forget to pay attention to the inner commitment part.*

commitment. I think that's all right. In fact, I think it's good.

The problem for me is that sometimes we get so busy working out the appearance part of our lives that we forget to pay attention to the inner commitment part, and we don't get as far as we should with the things that really matter the most. Worst of all is that there are people in this world who will fake the inner commitment by assuming the outward appearance. Appearance is shaky ground when it comes to forming judgments. And if you are using outward appearances as the basis for assessing your success as a mother, you are on particularly shaky ground because those appearances can change so quickly.

## THE SLOW-RIPENING FRUITS OF MOTHERING

Case in point: I am at the grocery store with my three-year-old daughter. She has the pint-sized grocery cart and is pushing it along beside me with my regular-sized cart. We are quite a picture, the two of us shopping together, me initiating my little girl into the mysteries of the grocery world. I can see it in the approving expressions of the shoppers passing us in Aisle 7: "Isn't that darling? What a lovely child. What a good mother."

Then we turn into Aisle 8, which is where the Oreos reside, right at the three-year-old's eye level. She chooses a package of cookies from the shelf and puts them in her cart. I pluck them out of the cart and return them to the shelf with a cheery if somewhat terse, "Not today, sweetheart. We're not going to buy those cookies today."

Well, perdition hath no fury like a three-year-old deprived of her Oreos, and she immediately flings herself to the ground and begins screaming. And I can see it in the disgusted expressions of the shoppers passing us in Aisle 8: "What a brat! Why doesn't her mother control her? Why would anyone bring a child like that out in public?"

Well, which is it? Angel child, or demon spawn? Am I a good mom or a bad mom? All too often, people will form that judgment depending on the moment in which they catch me at my mothering.

I want to grab the tantrum observers as they pass by and tell them that *this never works*. I never buy Oreos under coercion. I am a sensible, intelligent mother, with appropriate boundaries. But they have made their judgments based on what they see. Appearances. They can indeed be deceiving.

Here's a challenge, though: Don't the scriptures say, "By their fruits ye shall know them" (see Matthew 7:17; 3 Nephi 14:16)? They do. What they forget to remind us is that sometimes fruit takes a long time to ripen.

Think about this. Have you ever bitten into a fruit that's not ripe—a hard strawberry or a green melon or something like that? It's gross. All you really want to do is spit it out. If you were judging

# THE SLOW-RIPENING FRUITS OF MOTHERING

the fruit *based on that appearance at that time,* you might think the fruit was not good. But if you waited until the fruit was ripe and then tried it, you would see how delicious it could be.

>
> *An important thing to understand about raising children is that children are the slowest-ripening fruit there is.*

An important thing to understand about raising children is that children are the slowest-ripening fruit there is. Those precious fruits of our mothering take a long time to mature, and what's more, they all ripen at different rates. So it's unproductive and even dangerous to base our feelings of mothering confidence on where the fruit is at any given time.

We need to have a stronger foundation that we can build on, a stronger truth that doesn't bend with the wind or get tossed with the waves (see Ephesians

4:14; James 1:6). One such truth that has helped me a great deal as I've tried to cope with all my little slow-ripening fruits is this: "Heavenly Father loves my children as much as I do."

I remember the amazing feeling that came over me when I realized: This is God's child too; this isn't just my little one. This is Heavenly Father's child, and He loves him as much as I do. If you want to know how important that is to know, just think about how much you are affected when somebody mortal, right here on earth, loves your child even a little bit differently than you do, and how that helps give you perspective.

I want to share with you an experience I had

>
> *I remember the amazing feeling that came over me when I realized: This is God's child too; this isn't just my little one. This is Heavenly Father's child, and He loves him as much as I do.*

# THE SLOW-RIPENING FRUITS OF MOTHERING

with that. We have a child who lived out his elementary school days basically in an alternate dimension. His reality touched ours every now and then, but pretty much he lived elsewhere in his mind.

Someone said to me once, "I bet he has a rich inner life."

I said, "I sure hope so, because there isn't much outward life that I can see."

He was a fun kid, but he wasn't always easy to figure out. For example, when he was in kindergarten, his teacher said, "Dylan the bat comes to kindergarten more often than Dylan the child."

I said: "Oh, I'm so sorry. Is he disruptive? Is he hurting the class?"

"Oh, no, no. He just flutters everywhere he goes, and when we sit down on the rug for story time, he wraps his wings around him. Basically, he is all right; I just thought you might like to know."

Okay, great.

In first grade, his teacher had a policy that the kids brought up their papers at the end of class each day to be stapled together. That would give her a chance to see what they had worked on and tell them, "Great job." This teacher said to me at parent-teacher conference, "When Dylan brings his papers up, he is as surprised as you are to find that they are not completed. I say, 'Dylan, you didn't do this work,' and he says, 'I didn't?'"

I started paying closer attention, because this was child number four, and I wasn't getting to the bottom of the backpack very often anymore at this stage of my mothering career. So I tried to be more diligent about pulling those pages out, and sure enough—the work was often not done.

One day I said, "Dylan, why didn't you finish this work?"

He replied, "Greg had a new orange crayon in class today." (As if the presence of a new orange crayon in the classroom explained everything: How could anybody be expected to get their work done when there was a new orange crayon to be explored in the classroom?)

## THE SLOW-RIPENING FRUITS OF MOTHERING

We were in a little bit of despair about this child, but his teacher, who really liked him, said to me: "Listen, don't worry about Dylan. Dylan is a great kid and a smart kid. Information is getting in; it just doesn't go in the same way it does for most of us. But I don't want you to worry about him, because he is going to be just fine."

I started immediately to watch for evidences that this might actually be true. One day, we were driving in the car, and Sylvia, Dylan's little sister, said, "I'm cold."

Dylan shot right back, "If you were a lizard, you wouldn't be cold. Your body would be the same temperature as the air around it."

Another day, we were watching a favorite cartoon in which the little tiny characters were running around in a spiral up the carved leg of a giant table. And Dylan said, "Look, Mom, an inclined plane."

I thought, *His teacher's right! He really is learning stuff! He might not be putting it on his papers, but he's getting it.*

I can't tell you how much more relaxed I felt that somebody who knew my son in a different way could look at him and see what I couldn't. With her vast experience and knowledge about children, that teacher brought a different perspective to the picture and helped to reassure me that my son and I would be all right. I have always been grateful for her calm insight and understanding.

Now, suppose the person who is helping you see your child differently is Heavenly Father. Suppose He doesn't just like him as a student but loves him as a son, with a love that believes all things, and hopes all things, and endures all things (see 1 Corinthians 13:7). That kind of Being loves my little boy.

Will He help me have some perspective about that child and how to raise him? Yes, He does. He will. Will He give me insights of things that I could do as the steward, the mother of this boy, to help him realize his full potential? He can, He does, and He will. Will He smooth our way so that we don't have to fall over all these obstacles on the path? No,

## THE SLOW-RIPENING FRUITS OF MOTHERING

not always. And I'll tell you why—or at least one reason I have come to believe why.

One day when I was rereading the story of Joseph Smith in the Pearl of Great Price, I was particularly struck by some wording in the verse in which he's talking about his religious quest. He says in verse 8 of Joseph Smith–History, "During this time of great excitement"—religious excitement—"my mind was called up to serious reflection and great uneasiness; but though my feelings were deep and often poignant, still I kept myself aloof from all these parties, though I attended their several meetings as often as occasion would permit." At fourteen years old, his feelings were "deep and often poignant"? He was

*Now, suppose the person who is helping you see your child differently is Heavenly Father. Suppose He doesn't just like him as a student but loves him as a son.*

going to church as often as he could? Do you know a fourteen-year-old boy like that?

I thought, *What would make a fourteen-year-old boy do that kind of deep, serious, poignant soul-searching?* And then I remembered: When Joseph Smith was seven years old, typhoid fever had raged through the neighborhood and had hit the Smith family. In his case it had settled as an infection in his leg. Normally, the treatment would have been amputation, but his mother begged the doctors and prevailed upon them to try a relatively new procedure, which involved not taking off the whole leg but cutting out the portion of the bone that was infected. It just sounds hideous. I try to picture a child having such an operation without anesthesia, and I can't; my mind will not even go there. But that was how it was. Joseph was to undergo this operation, and he didn't want to take the whiskey that was the only option available to deaden his senses. He said, "If I can be held in the arms of my father, I'll be all right."

## THE SLOW-RIPENING FRUITS OF MOTHERING

It is interesting to me that he asked for his father, knowing his mother couldn't do it. In fact, this insightful little boy asked her to stay away altogether, and she wasn't in the room when the operation began.

When they cut into his leg to get to the bone, Joseph cried out so loudly that his mother came running into the room. She describes in her history the blood and carnage, the scene on the bed that she saw. And this seven-year-old boy called out: "Mother, go out. I will try to stand it if you will just go away." So she did, all the way out of the house into the orchard to pray.

Well, Joseph Smith survived that operation. He made it through that terrible, terrible ordeal, though it took years, and his brother Hyrum was the one, largely, who carried him around, who nursed him, who rubbed his leg when it hurt, who took care of him, forging a bond that would last all the way to Carthage jail, when they left the world together (see Lucy Mack Smith, *History of Joseph Smith*, 69–76).

I think that's where deep and serious and poignant feelings might have started for Joseph Smith. And when I see that, I understand better that Heavenly Father doesn't always take the hard things out of our path—because sometimes those trials are making us who we need to be. I am grateful to Him for that.

> *Heavenly Father doesn't always take the hard things out of our path—because sometimes those trials are making us who we need to be.*

Sometimes (usually in retrospect) I can really appreciate the purpose of my assorted trials and recognize the way they are helping me grow. At other times, especially when my challenges are self-inflicted, it's harder for me to see them as useful. I find myself wondering, *Why would Heavenly Father bother to fix this if I willfully stepped into the mess in*

## THE SLOW-RIPENING FRUITS OF MOTHERING

*the first place?* Do you ever feel like that? I get busy, I get tired, I get grumpy, I say things I shouldn't say, and I see that I am at fault. How can I ask Heavenly Father to be with me and help me through my trials if I'm the one who created those trials by my own actions?

A favorite little poem of mine, by an unknown author, helps me understand this better. It goes like this:

*With thoughtless and impatient hands*
*We tangle up the plans*
*The Lord hath wrought.*
*And when we cry in pain He saith,*
*"Be quiet, man, while I untie the knot."*

("With Thoughtless and Impatient Hands," in Lyon et al., *Best-Loved Poems,* 304)

Even when we are the ones who tangle up Heavenly Father's plans with our "thoughtless and impatient hands," He always invites us to be still and trust that He can undo the damage we have done. But we have to "be quiet" and let Him do His work.

> *I forget that Heavenly Father wants the mess. He wants the heart that's broken, not the one I've pridefully tried to piece together myself.*

This is hard for me. For many years I subscribed to the "Do-It-Yourself Salvation Plan," the basic tenet of which is that I will clean up my own messes and then, when I'm more presentable, I'll bring my offering to the altar. (This is the same mentality that prevents me from hiring much-needed help to clean my house. In order for me to have strangers in to clean, I'd have to do so much work cleaning up first that I figure I might just as well take it the rest of the way. What's wrong with that logic?)

I forget that Heavenly Father wants the mess. He wants the heart that's broken, not the one I've pridefully tried to piece together myself. Who am I kidding to think that He doesn't already know

## THE SLOW-RIPENING FRUITS OF MOTHERING

perfectly well how messy my life is? Jesus Christ already paid the price for all of the conditions of my mortality—my mistakes and my sins and my challenges and my heartbreaks. But He can't fix them if I don't turn them over to Him.

As with many of my questions about my relationship with my Heavenly Father, I turn to my own experiences as a mom to really understand this principle:

Have you ever had a child who had trouble getting his shoes on the right feet? I did. And he was a stubborn enough child that he never wanted me to change them even when they were obviously uncomfortable and possibly hazardous. In such a case, I could have just sat quietly and said to myself, "Well, he's messed it up again, and he doesn't even want help. I guess I'll leave him alone to figure it out on his own." But I never did that. I always tried my best, despite his resistance, to help him get his shoes on right, and ultimately, he was always happier once we got them straightened out.

Have you ever had a child like that? Do you ever stop wanting him to have his shoes on the right feet? Do you give up on him? Sometimes, if he simply won't listen, you just have to let him wear the shoes that way, but I submit that you always *want* to help. I think that's how it is with Heavenly Father. Sometimes, for whatever reason, we have a hard time listening, but He always wants to help. He never stops trying.

I went on a quest to try to understand better the truth that Heavenly Father is not just capable of helping me in my difficulties but willing and anxious to do so. I went to the heading *Trust* in the Topical Guide and found some wonderful scriptures that have helped me see things a little more clearly. The first one that I want to share with you is Psalm 27:14, which says: "Wait on the Lord: be of good courage, and he shall strengthen thine heart: wait, I say, on the Lord." This is not my favorite scripture because I have never been a very good waiter. It is

## THE SLOW-RIPENING FRUITS OF MOTHERING

not easy for me to have the courage it takes all along the way to wait for that child-fruit to ripen.

But waiting ultimately yields its rewards, little glimmers now and then that strengthen our hearts and give us hope that the fruit is coming along. That little girl who came to the grocery store with me occasionally (when I couldn't avoid it) is a good example of this. She has always had the blessing and the curse of knowing her own mind. The back of her bedroom door still bears the scars of where she used to kick it when she was in time out, learning to behave herself a little better. She wouldn't ever try to come out, but she would lie on her back on the floor and just kick the door.

Now, lest you think this child was entirely unmanageable, I have to reveal that she had a very logical brain and could often be reasoned with. Consider this sample conversation:

Child: "I want to go to Walmart."

Mom: "I'm sorry, honey, we are not going to go to Walmart today."

Child: "When *can* we go to Walmart?"

Mom: "Well, Saturday."

Child: "What time?"

Mom (picking a number out of the air): "Ten o'clock."

After such a conversation, she was pacified, and you wouldn't hear about Walmart the whole rest of the week. But on Saturday at ten o'clock you had better be at the back door with your keys in your hand, ready to go to Walmart. You promised. Never mind what might have come up in the meantime; she was willing to delay gratification but she is not going to be flexible about a promise you made. She knows what she wants. This quality made her—how should I put this?—not always the easiest child to live with.

Now I want to fast-forward to another era in this child's life. She is sixteen, and we are shopping for her first prom dress. If there is a more miserable experience on the planet . . . well, shopping for slacks for myself comes pretty close. But shopping for a

# THE SLOW-RIPENING FRUITS OF MOTHERING

modest prom dress, that is just a hard, frustrating thing to do. We had been to some stores and not had much success. Everything was strapless or backless or lacking in some other basic qualification that I generally look for in an item of clothing. We were getting worn out.

Then, in about the seventeenth store we entered, there on the clearance rack was a dress that looked like it might work. I held my breath and reached for the tag, and to my utter amazement, it was the right size. It was beautiful. It was sparkly. And it had sleeves. We grabbed the dress and practically ran to the dressing room.

When I zipped my daughter into it, you could almost hear the bells going off. It was as if this dress had been tailor-made for this girl. It enhanced her figure perfectly without being obnoxious about it. She looked so grown up, and the color was perfect with her eyes and her complexion, and I found myself getting kind of choked up with the emotion of it all: my last child, going to the prom in a great dress that was on clearance sale for—get this—*thirty-six dollars.*

One slight problem with the dress: It was a little bit low in the front. It was not immodest, truly, but it was lower than the tops she was used to wearing, and she was uncomfortable.

She said: "I don't know, Mom. I don't know if I can do it."

I'm thinking, *We have been everywhere in the city, and this dress is thirty-six dollars.*

Out loud, I said: "Honey, I promise it's fine." (Have you ever heard of a mother trying to talk her daughter *out* of being too modest? Yes, I was *that* mom that day.) "I promise it will be great."

She was wavering back and forth on the issue, and finally I came up with what seemed like an elegant solution. The dress had a silver sash, and I said, "What if we got some silver material that matched the sash of this, and we could just put some in the neckline to bring it up a little bit?"

## THE SLOW-RIPENING FRUITS OF MOTHERING

She said: "Okay, I can live with that. I think that will be all right."

So we bought the dress, and then we went straight to the fabric store to get the silver material so we could get right on this. We were lucky enough to find fabric that was almost a perfect match for the sash, so things were looking bright. We took it all home and got out the sewing machine, having forgotten to take into account the one little fact that I. Don't. Sew. I mean, I can work the treadle and push a piece of fabric along, but I am not a sewing mom. And this is not a case where duct tape is going to help. I have found duct tape to be very useful in some sewing instances, particularly when a long, tedious

*Have you ever heard of a mother trying to talk her daughter <u>out</u> of being too modest? Yes, I was <u>that</u> mom that day.*

hemming job stretches before me, but this was not one of those instances. I was cutting and shaping and sweating over the project (trying very hard not to speak aloud the less-than-appropriate words that were running through my head), but I wasn't really succeeding.

My daughter stepped in to try to help, and after quite a while spent messing with this thing that I thought was superfluous in the first place, I finally said to her, "Honey, are you sure we really need to do this?"

She answered, "I think if I were going with anyone but Chris, maybe it wouldn't matter so much, but I know he would be uncomfortable. Can we please keep trying?"

Wow.

Can I tell you how much I wanted to telephone Chris's mom right then and say: "Do you have any idea how ripe your fruit is? Do you have any idea how great it is that you have raised a son who makes my daughter want to be modest?" Because I don't

## THE SLOW-RIPENING FRUITS OF MOTHERING

know if she knew how amazing that was. And I'm quite sure *I* didn't know that a child who knows her own mind is exactly what the world needs in this difficult age, and that the personality trait that was so hard when she was two is what is going to make her a spectacular young woman and student and missionary and mom in her own right.

That fruit takes a long time to ripen. It takes a lot of faith, and a lot of spiritual insight and divine encouragement, to see it as it's really going to be. In the end, in order to have the patience we need, we have to remember how fruit ripens. Consider that we plant it, and we nurture it, and we water it, and we do what we can, but the ripening of that fruit is mostly up to the sun. It's the same with the fruit of our children. Ultimately, their maturing depends largely on the Son. We have to trust Him.

This leads me to a second scripture about trust. I need to credit the Topical Guide for leading me to this one because I don't really cruise through First Chronicles all that much in my regular scripture reading. It's great to be guided to scriptures that we might otherwise overlook but that have great messages. I really love this scripture. The Israelites were at war, as they often were, and the verse tells us, "They cried to God in the battle, and he was intreated of them; because they put their trust in him" (1 Chronicles 5:20).

*We plant it, and we nurture it, and we water it, and we do what we can, but the ripening of that fruit is mostly up to the sun. It's the same with the fruit of our children. Ultimately, their maturing depends largely on the Son. We have to trust Him.*

Do you ever think that being a parent is a battle? I submit that moms have to fight lots of battles, big and little. When I think of that scripture, I think of one mother I knew who had a particularly difficult battle. She was a single mother who had not always

## THE SLOW-RIPENING FRUITS OF MOTHERING

been active in the Church, but was now trying her best to raise her children with the light of the gospel. She had recently been through the temple and was renewed in her determination to help them have the blessings she had missed in her early adulthood. And then she learned that her beautiful fourteen-year-old daughter—we'll call her Suzy—was pregnant.

There was a lot of crying to God in that battle, as you can imagine. That mother wept and prayed and tried to help her daughter see that her baby could be adopted by a wonderful couple who would give him a great life, but in the end Suzy made the decision to marry the baby's father. This was a heartbreaking decision for my friend because she knew what kind of a boy that father was.

After a few years, one or two more children, and a long string of abuse, Suzy finally developed the strength to extricate herself from that untenable situation and got divorced. Then my friend moved away, and I pretty much lost track of the family.

Some years later, my friend called me unexpectedly.

I'd never heard her sound happier. She said, "I just thought you might like to know that Suzy was called last week as Young Women president in her ward."

I thought, *There was a mom who trusted God and cried to Him in the battle, and He was intreated of her.* I'm certain that Heavenly Father put experiences slowly, incrementally, gradually in Suzy's path to help her come back to where she needed to be. I'm also quite sure that Suzy wasn't the one who was praying for those experiences. It was her mom's prayers that the Lord was answering (at least to begin with). That knowledge gives me a lot of hope as a mother.

I love the words of the hymn:
*And when the strife is fierce, the warfare long,*
*Steals on the ear the distant triumph song,*
*And hearts are brave again, and arms are strong.*
("For All the Saints," *Hymns*, no. 82)

That's what crying to God in the battle means to me.

I have one more scripture and one more story

## THE SLOW-RIPENING FRUITS OF MOTHERING

to share about trusting the Lord. The scripture is Psalm 9:10: "And they that know thy name will put their trust in thee: for thou, Lord, hast not forsaken them that seek thee."

*And they that know thy name will put their trust in thee: for thou, Lord, hast not forsaken them that seek thee. —Psalm 9:10*

The story is about another friend of mine, a man who knew the voice of the Lord and trusted Him. This was one of the really good men of my acquaintance; he had held many positions of responsible leadership in the Church and was very spiritually attuned but never, ever to the point of taking himself too seriously. He had a great, quirky sense of humor and was a lot of fun to be around.

This man had a son, his only son, who had been introduced to drugs in elementary school by the sort of unscrupulous people that make you weep over the power of Satan on this earth. My friend's family had had all kinds of trouble throughout the years as they tried to help their boy break the grip of his terrible addiction. They tried everything, including making the heartbreaking choice that he could no longer live under their roof. When he hit the bottom (and the conditions in which he was living were a parent's worst nightmare), he humbled himself and asked to come back home, and they brought him back. He was in his thirties by this time.

He was fighting the good fight, and seeing some success. There was a glimmer of hope for probably the first time in many years for these great parents. And then they went down to his room one morning and found him dead of an overdose.

No one knows, or will ever know, exactly what happened there, though the assumption was that it was an accident. But that doesn't really matter. The unimaginably difficult fact was that their son was

## THE SLOW-RIPENING FRUITS OF MOTHERING

gone. The searing pain of that is almost more than I can get my mind around.

I would think that my friend, in that moment, *could* have felt forsaken by the Lord. He might have felt that everything he had done was in vain. But he came to know in a very personal way, and I testify to you that it's true, that there were people even now working with his son on the other side of the veil to help him come to the understanding that he never was able to achieve in this mortal life.

That is another bit of insight that I need as a mother: Sometimes the fruit doesn't ripen on this side of the veil. Sometimes it takes clear into the next life for things to get worked out, but if we trust in the

*By our fruits we will be known. But not now. Not yet. We need to give ourselves time, and give our children time.*

Lord, He does not forsake us. He never will. He has promised as much.

By our fruits we will be known. But not now. Not yet. We need to give ourselves time, and give our children time.

One last thought regarding this principle occurred to me when I was pondering it one day: What if the fruit of my parenting isn't my children at all? What if the fruit of me being a mom is who *I* am becoming as a result of being that parent?

*What if the fruit of my parenting isn't my children at all? What if the fruit of me being a mom is who I am becoming as a result of being that parent?*

That thought changes the whole picture. I start to realize that the children who are the hardest are very often the ones who are making *me* the most of who I need to be. The problem children (and they're all problem

## THE SLOW-RIPENING FRUITS OF MOTHERING

children at some point, I think) are the ones who drive me to the arms of the Savior. They're the ones whose challenges put me on my knees to ask their Father, "Thou who lovest this child more than I do, wilt Thou help me understand what I need to do to bring him back to Thee?"

The fruit of my life is me, and most of what I know about believing all things and hoping all things and enduring all things (see 1 Corinthians 13:7), I have learned as a result of being a mom. To me, the most interesting thing about that is that I have friends who would say that everything they know about believing and hoping and enduring has come to them because they haven't yet had a chance to be a mom. Isn't it amazing how Heavenly Father takes the circumstances of our mortality and uses them to mold us and make us who we need to be to return to Him?

I leave you my testimony that He loves you individually, just as He loves your children individually, that you are His precious daughter, and that He will give to you the capacity to be who He needs you to be and who you need to be to return to Him. I testify of that reality with all of my heart and with the great joy that it is to know the truth of the gospel.

## Sources

*Hymns of The Church of Jesus Christ of Latter-day Saints.* Salt Lake City: The Church of Jesus Christ of Latter-day Saints, 1985.

Lyon, Jack M., Linda Ririe Gundry, Jay A. Parry, and Devan Jensen, compilers. *Best-Loved Poems of the LDS People.* Salt Lake City: Deseret Book, 1996.

Smith, Lucy Mack. *The Revised and Enhanced History of Joseph Smith by His Mother.* Scot Facer Proctor and Maurine Jensen Proctor, editors. Salt Lake City: Deseret Book, 1996.